MW01521003

Edited by
Vicki Brown

Cover Design by
Gary Will - dba Advent Designs

Printed by
The Barr Company
Fort Worth, Texas

ISBN 0-9712097-2-3

Table of Contents

The Bible, God's Word

2 Peter 1:21 ---------------------------- What is the origin of the Bible?

John 17:17 ---------------------------- What did Jesus call God's word?

2 Timothy 3:16, 17 --------------- How much of the Bible is inspired?

Psalm 119:105 -------------------- What is the word of God to be to us?

Romans 15:4 ----------------------------- Why was the Bible written?

1 Corinthians 10:11 -------------------- Why were the stories recorded?

John 20:31 ------ What is the ultimate reason the Bible was written?

John 5:39 ------------------------- What are we to do with it Scripture?

Isaiah 28:10 ------------------------------- How are we to study it?

2 Timothy 2:15 ------------------------- How are we to handle it?

2 Peter 3:16 --------------- What do some people do with God's word?

2 Peter 1:20 ----------------------------- What must we never do?

Acts 17:11 ------------------------ How often should we study the Bible?

2 Timothy 3:15-17 --------------------- What will Bible study do for us?

1 Corinthians 2:13, 14 ------------------ Why is it hard to understand?

John 16:13 --------------------------- Who will guide us in Bible study?

Proverbs 2:1-5 --------------------- How do we receive understanding?

The God of the Bible

Psalm 14:1 ------------------------------- Who says "there is no God"?
Genesis 1:1 ----------------------- What does the Bible say about God?
Isaiah 45:18 -------------------------- How many other gods are there?
Psalm 90:2 ------------------------------- How long has God existed?
1 Kings 8:30 ------------------------------------ Where does He dwell?
Psalm 19:1 ----------------------- What evidences do we see of God?
Isaiah 46:9, 10 ----------------------- What is He alone able to do?
1 John 4:8 ------------------------- What is God's greatest attribute?
John 3:16 ---------------------------------- How great is His love?
Romans 5:8 ------------------------------ When did God first love us?
Jeremiah 31:3 ------------------------- How long will He love us?
Romans 8:38, 39 ------------- What can separate us from God's love?
Isaiah 45:22 ---------------------------- What does He want us to do?
John 17:3 -------------------- How important is it that we know God?
1 John 3:1 --------------------------- What does He want us to become?
John 1:12, 13 --------------------------------------- How can we do this?
Romans 8:14-16 ---------------------- Who will lead us to our Father?

Jesus, the Son of God

The Holy Spirit

John 16:7 ------------------------------ Who did Jesus promise to send?
John 16:8-15 ----------------------------- What will the Holy Spirit do?
John 14:26 ----------------------- What else will He do for the believer?
Acts 5:32 ------------------------------ To whom is the Holy Spirit given?
Luke 11:9-13 -------------- How willing is God to give us His Spirit?
Romans 5:5 ----------------------— What does He place in our hearts?
John 3:5 ----------------------- How important is receiving the Spirit?
Romans 8:1, 9 --------------- What is our condition without the Spirit?
Romans 8:14-16 -------------- What assurance does the Spirit bring?
Galatians 5:16, 17 ------- Will one sin who is being led of the Spirit?
Ephesians 4:30 ------------------------ What should we seek not to do?
Genesis 6:3 --------------- What happens when we grieve the Spirit?
Romans 8:13 -------------------- What is God's warning and promise?
Galatians 6:7, 8 ---------------------------- What does a person reap?
Luke 11:9-13 --------------------- How do we receive the Holy Spirit?

The Plan of Salvation

Matthew 1:21 ----------------------------------- Why did Jesus come?

Isaiah 59:2 ------------------------------------ What does sin do?

Romans 6:23 --------------------------------- What is the result of sin?

Ezekiel 18:4 ---------------------------------- What happens to sinners?

Romans 3:23 ---------------------------------- How many have sinned?

Romans 5:12 --------------------------------- How many are to die?

Jeremiah 13:23 ------------------------------ Can we change ourselves?

2 Peter 3:9 ----------------------------------- What are God's feelings?

John 3:16 ----------------------------- What provision did He make?

Romans 5:8 --------------------------------- When did He first love us?

Ephesians 2:8, 9 --------------------------------- How are we saved?

What does this saving faith produce in our lives?

Luke 5:32 --- Repentance.

1 John 1:9 --- Confession.

Proverbs 28:13 -- Forsaking.

Matthew 7:21 -- Obedience.

2 Corinthians 6:2 -------------------- When should we accept this gift?

John 1:12 --------------------------------- What do we become?

The New Birth

Romans 7:18, 19 ------------------- Have you ever experienced this?

Romans 7:20 -------------------- What is the cause of this condition?

Romans 8:7, 8 ----------------------------------- What causes us to sin?

Romans 8:6 -------------------- What is the result of the carnal mind?

Romans 7:24, 25 ----------------------------------- Who can rescue us?

Philippians 4:13 ---------------------- What can Jesus enable us to do?

Galatians 2:20 --------------------------- What makes this possible?

Romans 6:1-6 ---------------------- What type of a life do we now live?

2 Corinthians 5:15, 17 ---------------------- How new is this life to be?

John 3:1-8 ----------------------------------- What is this life likened to?

Romans 8:1, 9, 14 ------------------ How important is this new birth?

Ephesians 4:22-24 ---------------------- What is the new person like?

Philippians 2:13 -------------------------------- How is this possible?

The Origin of the Earth

Genesis 1:1 ----------------------------------- Who created the earth?

Genesis 1:26 ----------------------------- What does "let us" indicate?

Genesis 1:2 ------------------------- Who else was involved in creation?

Hebrews 1:2 --------------------------- Who actually did the creating?

John 1:1-3, 14 --------------------------- How much did He create?

Psalm 33:6-9 --- How did He create?

Isaiah 45:18 ---------------------------- Why did He create the earth?

Exodus 20:11 ---------------------------- How long did creation take?

Hebrews 11:3 ------------------------ What enables us to accept this?

Colossians 1:16, 17 ---------------------------- Who sustains the world?

2 Peter 3:3-5 --------------- What would people doubt in the last days?

Revelation 14:7 --------------- Whom are we called upon to worship?

The Second Coming of Christ

John 14:1-3 ----------------------------- What did Jesus promise to do?

Acts 1:9-11 ------------------------------------- How will He come?

Luke 24:36-43, 50, 51 ----------------------------- Was He a real person?

Will His coming be visible, audible, and personal?

Matthew 24:27 --------------------- To what does He liken His coming?

Matthew 24:30 ----------------- What type of glory accompanies Him?

Luke 9:26 --- Whose glory is it?

Matthew 24:31 --------------------------------- What do the angels do?

1 Thessalonians 4:16, 17 --------------------- What happens to the dead?

Revelation 6:14-17 ---- What happens to the islands and mountains?

Revelation 16:17-21 ---- What 100 pound objects desolate the earth?

Revelation 1:7 ------------------------- How many will see Him coming?

John 14:1-3 --------------------------------- Why is Jesus coming back?

Signs of the Second Coming

Matthew 24:3 ------------------------------ What did the disciples ask?

Matthew 24:4, 5 --------------------- What did Jesus say would come?

Matthew 24:6 ------------------------------ What will we hear about?

Matthew 24:7 ----------- What will be happening in different places?

Matthew 24:11 --------------------- Who shall arise and deceive many?

Matthew 24:12 ---------- What two signs are evident in society today?

Matthew 24:13 ----------------------------- What assurance is given to us?

Matthew 24:14 ---------------------------- What is to go to all the world?

Daniel 12:4 ---------------------------------- What would be increased?

2 Timothy 3:1 ----------- What kind of times did He say would come?

2 Timothy 3:2 ---------------------------- What eight signs are given?

2 Timothy 3:3 -- Another six signs.

2 Timothy 3:4, 5 -- Six more signs.

2 Peter 3:3, 4 ---------- What kind of people did He say would come?

2 Peter 3:5, 6 --------------- What two other things would they reject?

Matthew 24:21, 22 -- What type of tribulation precedes His coming?

Revelation 6:12-14 -------------- What four signs precede His coming?

Matthew 24:29-33 -------------------- What is the next thing to happen?

Matthew 24:36 ---------------------------- Do we know the exact time?

Matthew 24:42, 44 ------------------ What are we to do while waiting?

Death

Genesis 2:7 ---------------------------------- What did Adam become?

Ecclesiastes 3:20 ---------------------------------- Who returns to dust?

Ecclesiastes 12:7 ------------------------ Whose spirit returns to God?

Job 27:3 -- What is the spirit?

Psalm 104:29 ----- What does God take that turns the body to dust?

Job 14:10 -------------------------- What age old question did Job ask?

Job 14:12 ----------------------------------- What is the Bible answer?

Job 14:21 ------------- Do the dead know what happens to the living?

Ecclesiastes 9:5, 6, 10 ------------------- How much do the dead know?

Psalm 146:1-4 ------------------------- When are we to praise the Lord?

Psalm 115:17 ----------------------------- Do the dead praise the Lord?

Psalm 6:5 ---------------------------- Can the dead even remember God?

John 11:11-14 ---------------------------------- What did Jesus call death?

John 11:17 ---------------------------- How long had Lazarus been dead?

John 11:20-27 ----------- Did Martha believe Lazarus was in heaven?

John 11:32-35 -- What did Mary say?

John 11:39, 40 ----------- Why didn't Martha want the stone moved?

John 11:43, 44 --- Was Lazarus called from heaven, hell, or the grave?

1 Corinthians 15:16-23 ---------------------- When are the dead raised?

1 Corinthians 15:51-55 ------------ When do we receive immortality?

1 Thessalonians 4:13-18 ------------------------ Our hope and comfort.

The Origin and Destiny of Satan

Why did Jesus come to this world?

1 John 3:5 -------------------------- What did Jesus come to take away?

John 3:16 ---------------------------------- What did He come to give?

1 John 3:8 ------------------------------ What did He come to destroy?

Hebrews 2:14 -------------------------- Whom did He come to destroy?

Can Satan be destroyed?

1 Timothy 6:16 ---------------------------------- Who only is immortal?

Luke 10:18 ------------------------------ Where did Satan come from?

Ezekiel 28:12-15 -- What was he?

Ezekiel 28:16 -- What did he do?

Isaiah 14:12-14 -- What was his sin?

Revelation 12:7-9 -------------- What was the result of his rebellion?

Genesis 3:1-6 -- What did he do?

1 Peter 5:8 -- What does he want?

Revelation 12:12 ---------------------------- Why is he working so hard?

Ezekiel 28:17-19 ------------------------------ What will happen to him?

Ephesians 6:11-17 ---------------------------- How can we defeat him?

James 4:7 -------------------- What two things will guarantee victory?

The Punishment of the Wicked

John 3:16 -------------------------- What is the opposite of eternal life?

Romans 6:23 ------------------------------- What is the wages of sin?

Ezekiel 18:4 ----------------------- What becomes of the soul that sins?

1 Peter 5:8 --------------------------------- What does the devil want?

Revelation 12:12 --------------------------------- How long does he have?

Ezekiel 28:18-19 --------------------------- What will happen to him?

Psalm 37:20 --------------------------------- What about his followers?

Matthew 10:28 --------------- What happens to body and soul in hell?

Malachi 4:1-3 ---------------------------- What do the wicked become?

Revelation 20:14 ------------------------- What is the lake of fire called?

Revelation 21:8 --------------------------------- Who will be cast there?

2 Peter 3:10-12 --------------------------------- What else is destroyed?

2 Peter 3:13 --------------------------------- What are we to look for?

Revelation 21:1 ------------------------------------- What did John see?

Revelation 21:3, 4 -------------------------- What is God's promise?

Revelation 21:5 ------------------------- Can we trust this promise?

The Millennium

Isaiah 24:1, 3, 20 ----- What happens to the earth when Jesus comes?

Revelation 6:14 -------- What becomes of the islands and mountains?

Jeremiah 4:23-27 --------------- How desolate will the earth become?

Jeremiah 25:30-33 ------------------ What happens to all of the wicked?

1 Thessalonians 4:15-17 --------- What happens to the righteousness?

> *NOTE: When Jesus comes the wicked are all slain, the righteous all taken to heaven, and the earth left in a desolate state ("without form and void" Jer. 4:23; as a "bottomless pit" Rev. 20:1).*

Revelation 20:1-3 ------------- How long is Satan bound to the earth?

Revelation 20:4 ----------------------- What will the righteous be doing?

1 Corinthians 6:2, 3 ---------------------- Whom shall they be judging?

John 5:28, 29 ------------- What did Jesus say about the resurrection?

Revelation 20:5, 6 ------------------ When are the wicked dead raised?

Revelation 20:7, 8 ------- What does Satan do when they are raised?

Revelation 21:2 ------------------------- What descends down from God?

Revelation 20:9 -------- What does Satan attempt and what happens?

Psalm 37:20 ------------------------------ How consuming is this fire?

Malachi 4:1-3 ------------------------------ What do the wicked become?

Ezekiel 28:18, 19 ------------------------------ What becomes of Satan?

Revelation 20:14 ---------------------------------- What is this fire called?

2 Peter 3:10-13 ------------------- What will God create from the ashes?

Revelation 21:1 ------------------------------- What did John see in vision?

Isaiah 65:17, 21-25 ------------------- What will the new earth be like?

Revelation 21:3-5 ------------------------------- What does God promise?

The Law of God

Romans 3:20 ---------------------- What is the purpose of God's law?

1 John 3:4 -- What is sin?

Romans 4:15 ---------------------- Can there be sin without the law?

Genesis 4:7-11 ---------------------------- What sin did Cain commit?

Genesis 13:13 ----------------- What were the people of Sodom called?

Genesis 26:5 ------------------- Did Abraham keep the commandments?

Genesis 39:9 ------- What commandment would Joseph have broken?

Exodus 16:4 -------------------- What did God test Israel to discover?

Exodus 16:23-28 -------- Did they sin or obey God's commandment?

Note: This experience took place two weeks before God wrote the ten commandments in Exodus Chapter 20.

Exodus 31:18 ----------------- How were the commandments written?

Matthew 5:17-19 ------------------------- Did Jesus change the law?

Romans 3:31 ---------------------------- Does faith abolish God's law?

Revelation 14:12 ------------- Who are the faithful when Jesus comes?

Psalm 111:7, 8 ------------- How long will His commandments stand?

John 14:15, 21, 23 ----------------- How do we show our love for God?

The Two Laws

Exodus 31:18 ----------------- How were the commandments written?

Exodus 25:16 ----------------------------- Where were they placed?

2 Chronicles 5:10 ------------------------ What else was placed there?

Psalm 111:7, 8 ---------- How long are these commandments to last?

Deuteronomy 31:24-26 ------- Where was the ceremonial law placed?

Hebrews 9:10 ------------------------------ How long was it to stand?

Ephesians 2:15 -------- What did the law that was abolished contain?

Colossians 2:14 ------------------------------- What was blotted out?

Deuteronomy 31:24-26 ----------------------- Who wrote this law?

Hebrews 7:26, 27; 9:11, 12 ----- To what did these ordinances point?

Daniel 9:27 ------------------------- What was to cease when Jesus died?

Matthew 27:50, 51 ----------------- What happened when Jesus died?

John 15:9, 10 -------------------- How are we to continue in His love?

1 John 2:3, 4 ------------ What if we do not keep His commandments?

Revelation 21:8 ------------------------------ What happens to all liars?

Revelation 22:14 --------- Where will the commandment keepers be?

The Bible Sabbath

Revelation 1:10 ---------- Does this verse say which day is the Lord's?

Mark 2:28 ----------------------- Which day did Jesus say is His day?

Isaiah 58:13 --------------------------- What did God call the Sabbath?

Exodus 20:8-11 ----------------------- Which day is the Bible Sabbath?

Genesis 2:1-3 ------------------- When was it sanctified and made holy?

Luke 23:52-56; 24:1 ----- What day of the week follows the Sabbath?

    NOTE: The Sabbath is the day between Good Friday and Easter Sunday, or Saturday, the seventh day of the week.

Mark 2:27 ----------------------- Was the Sabbath made for the Jews?

Luke 4:16 ----------------------------------- Did Jesus keep the Sabbath?

Acts 17:2 ----------------------------------- Did Paul keep the Sabbath?

Acts 13:42 ------------------- Did Gentile Christians keep the Sabbath?

Acts 13:44 ----------------------- How many were keeping the Sabbath?

Acts 16:13 ----------------------- When did Paul meet with the women?

Acts 18:4 ---------------------------- How often did they keep the Sabbath?

Matthew 24:20 ---------- What was Jesus' prayer for 40 years future?

Matthew 5:17, 18 ----- Did Jesus change any of the commandments?

Hebrews 4:3, 4, 9-11 ------------ Does the Sabbath rest remain today?

Exodus 20:8 ----- What word reveals man would forget the Sabbath?

Isaiah 66:22, 23 --------- Will the Sabbath be kept in the New Earth?

Ezekiel 20:12, 19, 20 ------ Who is the Sabbath to be a sign between?

Acts 5:29 ------------------------------------ Should we obey God or man?

Matthew 4:10 ----------------------- Who did Jesus say we should serve?

Romans 6:16 ------------------------------ What two choices do we have?

Joshua 24:14, 15 ----------------------------------- What are we told to do?

Joshua 24:24 ------------------------------- What should our response be?

Sunday in the New Testament

There are only eight texts in the entire New Testament that refer to the first day of the week. This study will consider each of them.

Matthew 28:1 ------------------------- Why did they come to the tomb?

Mark 16:1-2 -------------------- Were they coming to worship or work?

Mark 16:9 ----------- Does this verse say Jesus changed the Sabbath?

Mark 16:10-14 --------------- Were they celebrating the resurrection?

Luke 24:1 ------------ Does this verse indicate a change of God's law?

John 20:1 -------- Does this say the Sabbath was changed to Sunday?

John 20:19 ------------------------------------ Why were they assembled?

Acts 20:7-10 -------------------------- Why were there "many lights"?

> *NOTE: This is a Saturday night meeting that continued until dawn on Sunday.*

Acts 20:11, 14 ------- What did Paul do at dawn on Sunday morning?

> *NOTE: Paul preached till dawn Sunday and then walked 20 miles to Assos, something he would never have done on the holy Sabbath.*

1 Corinthians 16:1-2 ------ Does taking an offering make a day holy?

> *NOTE: Paul informed all of the churches, including Corinth, of the need of laying aside money at home for the poor believers in Jerusalem so that when he passed through he could readily pick it up to take to them. (See Acts 11:29, 30; Romans 15:25, 26.)*

Exodus 20:8 ----------------- What does the fourth commandment say?

Matthew 15:3, 6, 9 --------- What results from rejecting God's law?

John 14:15 ------------------------ What should we do if we love Jesus?

Love and Obedience

2 John 1:4-6 ------------------------- What are God's people to walk in?

2 Timothy 3:5 -------- What warning is given about some Christians?

2 Timothy 4:3, 4 ------------- What will some last day Christians do?

Romans 3:28 --- How are we saved?

Romans 3:31 ------------------------------- Does faith abolish the law?

James 2:17-20, 26 ----------------------- Faith without works is what?

Galatians 5:6 ------------------------------------ How does faith work?

Ezekiel 33:31 --------------------- Is more required than "lip service"?

James 1:22-25 --------------------- Who is deceived and who is blessed?

Hebrews 5:9 -------------------------------------- Who receives salvation?

Matthew 19:16, 17 -------------------- What did Jesus say we must do?

James 2:10-12 - What happens if we break even one commandment?

Matthew 7:21-23 ----------------------- What are the disobedient told?

Matthew 7:24-27 -------------------- Who are the wise and the foolish?

2 Thessalonians 1:7-9 ------------- What happens to the disobedient?

John 14:15 ----------------------- What is obedience an expression of?

1 John 2:3, 4 --------------------------------- Who does God call a liar?

Revelation 21:8 ------------------------ Where will ALL liars be found?

Revelation 22:14 --------- Where will the commandment keepers be?

Sabbath Observance

Exodus 20:10, 11 --------------------------- Which day is the Sabbath?

Mark 2:27 --------------------------- Who was the Sabbath made for?

Mark 2:28 ----------------------------------- Whose day is the Sabbath?

Isaiah 58:13 --------------------------- What does God call the Sabbath?

Leviticus 23:32 --------------------- When is the Sabbath to be observed?

Genesis 1:5, 8, 13 ----------------- What marks the beginning of a day?

Mark 6:2 --------------------------- What did Jesus do on the Sabbath?

Luke 4:16 ------------------------------ Was this His common practice?

Matthew 12:10-15 ---------- What else should one do on the Sabbath?

Isaiah 56:2 ---------------------- What brings God's promised blessing?

Exodus 20:8 ----------------------- What are we to "remember" to do?

Exodus 20:9-11 -------- What are we to refrain from on the Sabbath?

Nehemiah 13:15-18 ------- Why were the Jews carried into captivity?

Hebrews 4:9-11 ----------------------- What are we to learn from this?

Isaiah 56:6 --- If one is truly "joined" to God, what will they not do?

Isaiah 58:12 ----------------------------- What does God want us to be?

Isaiah 58:13 ----------------------------------- How only is this possible?

Isaiah 58:14 --- What is His promise?

Baptism

John 3:5 ------------------------------------- How essential is baptism?

Ephesians 4:5 ---- How many types of baptism does God recognize?

Matthew 3:13-17 --------------------------- How was Jesus baptized?

John 3:23 ------------------------------- Why did John baptize there?

Acts 8:38 --------------------- How did Philip baptize the Ethiopian?

Matthew 28:19, 20 ---------------------- What must precede baptism?

Mark 16:16 --------------------------------- What else must take place?

Acts 2:37, 38, 41 ----------------------------- What must follow belief?

Romans 6:3-6 --------------------------- What does baptism symbolize?

Galatians 2:20 ------------------------------------- Who now lives in us?

Galatians 3:26-29 ----------------------- What are we declared to be?

2 Corinthians 6:2 ------------------------- When should we be baptized?

Acts 19:1-5 ---------------- For what reason might one be rebaptized?

Acts 22:16 --------------------------------------- What should one not do?

The True Church

Ephesians 4:4-6 ------- How many bodies does God recognize as His?

Ephesians 1:22, 23 ---------------------------------- What is this body?

Revelation 12:1, 2 --- What symbol is used to portray God's church?

Jeremiah 6:2 -------------------------------- What is Zion compared to?

Isaiah 51:16 --- Who is Zion?

Revelation 17:1-5 ------ To what are the corrupt churches compared?

Revelation 12:3, 9 ---------- Who is this beast which carries Babylon?

Revelation 12:13 ----------------------- Whom does the devil persecute?

Revelation 12:14-16 --------- How long did the church go into hiding?

> *NOTE: For more information on the "1260 days" (vs. 6) and "time, and times, and half a time" (vs. 14) being the 1260 years of persecution from 538 to 1798, see the study on "The 1260 Years of Persecution."*

Revelation 12:17 --- How is the last day, remnant church identified?

Revelation 19:10 ----------------------- What is the testimony of Jesus?

> *NOTE: Several identifying marks of the remnant, or true church: 1. To keep all of the commandments of God; including the fourth, or the seventh day Sabbath (Rev. 12:17, 14:12). 2. To have the faith of Jesus (Rev. 14:12). 3. To have the testimony of Jesus, which is the spirit of prophecy (Rev. 12:17). 4. To arise after the 1260 years of persecution, or after 1798 (Rev. 12:14). 5. To proclaim the three angels' messages (Rev. 14:6-12). 6. To be a world-wide movement (Rev. 14:6). 7. To base all of their beliefs upon the Bible and the Bible alone (John 14:23-24, Rev. 22:18-19). 8. To identify and oppose the antichrist. 9. Not to be an offspring of Babylon (Rev. 17:5). 10. To call God's people out of Babylon (Rev. 18:4).*

Revelation 18:1-5 -------------- What is God's last call to His people?

John 10:16 ---------------------------------- Where are they to come to?

John 10:27 ------------------------- What does Jesus say His sheep do?

John 10:28 ------------ What is His promise to those who follow Him?

The Spirit of Prophecy

Revelation 12:17 ----- What two things identify the remnant church?

Revelation 19:10 ----------------------— What is the testimony of Jesus?

Amos 3:7 --------------------------- What is the purpose of a prophet?

NOTE: Three common misconceptions are: 1. To be a prophet one had to write a book of the Bible. Such a fallacy as this is easily refuted by such well known prophets as Elijah, John the Baptist, and dozens of others who did not write any of the Bible. 2. That the gift of prophecy ended with the death of the last of the apostles and the close of the New Testament. 3. That the prophetic gift was given to men only.

Ephesians 4:11-13 ---------- How long is this gift to be in the church?
Was this gift bestowed upon men only?

Exodus 15:20 --------------------------------------- What is Miriam called?

Judges 4:4 -------------------- In addition to Judge what was Deborah?

2 Chronicles 34:22 ---- Was the gift given to Hulda or her husband?

Acts 21:9 -------------- How many of Philip's daughters had the gift?

Joel 2:28-31 --------------------- Will this still happen in the last days?

Matthew 7:15-20 ---------- How can one tell the true from the false?

Jeremiah 28:9 ------------------------ Will what they say come to pass?

2 Peter 1:20 --- Do they place their own interpretation on Scripture?

Isaiah 8:20 ----------- Will all they say be in harmony with the Bible?

Isaiah 58:1 --------------------------------------- Will they point out sin?

1 Corinthians 14:3, 4 --------------------- Will they edify and counsel?

Isaiah 24:20 ------------------------------ Will they warn of judgment?

Deuteronomy 18:18-22 -------------- What if we reject a true prophet?

2 Chronicles 20:20 ---------------------- What is God's assurance to us?

1 Thessalonians 5:19-21 ----------------- What are we counseled to do?

26

Prayer

Philippians 4:6 ------------------------------- What are we told to do?
Luke 18:1 ----------------------------------- How often are we to pray?
John 16:23 ------------------------------------ Who are we to pray to?
Matthew 6:7 ---------------------- What should we not use in prayer?
Matthew 6:9-13 ---------- Did Jesus give an example of how to pray?
Matthew 7:7-11 -------------------------- What does He promise to do?
Mark 11:24 ------------- What must we do for prayer to be answered?
James 1:5-7 ----------------------------------- How essential is faith?
Matthew 26:39, 42 ----------------- Whose will should we be seeking?
1 John 5:14, 15 -------------------------- What assurance do we have?
James 4:3 ---------------------- Why are some prayers not answered?
Psalm 66:18 --- Does anything prevent God from hearing your prayer?
Isaiah 59:1, 2 ------------------------------------- What does sin do?
2 Chronicles 7:14 ----------------- What must we do for God to hear?
1 Peter 4:7 ------------------ Why is prayer so very important today?
Luke 21:36 --------------------------------- What should we be doing?

A Great Image

Daniel 2

Daniel 2:31 ----------------------- What did the king see in his dream?

Daniel 2:32, 33 -------------------------------- What did it look like?

Daniel 2:34-36 ---------------------------------- What happened to it?

Daniel 2:37, 38 ---------------- What did the golden head represent?

Daniel 2:39 ----------- What was represented by the silver and brass?

Daniel 5:28 ------------------------ What kingdom followed Babylon?

Daniel 8:20, 21 - What kingdom overthrew the Medes and Persians?

Daniel 2:40 ---- What metal represented the fourth kingdom, Rome?

Daniel 2:41, 42 ---- What was represented by the iron and clay feet?

> *NOTE: The 10 toes of this image represent the Saxons, Franks, Alemanni, Burgundians, Visigoths, Suevi, Lombards, Ostrogoths, Vandals, and Heruli.*

Daniel 2:43 ----------- What will these 10 kingdoms not be able to do?

Daniel 2:44 ------------------- What kingdom will rule the world next?

Daniel 2:45 --------------------------- How reliable is this prophecy?

Four Strange Beasts

Daniel 7

Daniel 7:1-3 -------------------------------------- What did Daniel see?

Jeremiah 51:1-4 ------------------------- What do "winds" represent?

Revelation 17:15 ------------------------ What does water symbolize?

Daniel 7:17-23 ----------------------------- What are the four "beasts"?

NOTE: These four beasts represent the same four kingdoms as the four metals of the image of Daniel 2.

Daniel 7:4 ----------- How is the first kingdom of Babylon portrayed?

Daniel 7:5 -------------------------------- How is Medo-Persia described?

Daniel 7:6 ----------------- What symbol is used to represent Greece?

Daniel 7:7, 23 --------------- What is the kingdom of Rome said to be?

NOTE: The 10 horns represent the same 10 kingdoms as the 10 toes of Daniel 2 which are the Saxons, Franks, Alemanni, Burgundians, Visigoths, Suevi, Lombards, Ostrogoths, Vandals, and Heruli.

Daniel 7:8 ------------------- What came up among these 10 kingdoms?

Daniel 7:24 ----------------------------- What would this little horn do?

Daniel 7:21 -- What else would it do?

Daniel 7:25 -------------------- What are three more things it would do?

Daniel 7:25 ---------------------------- How long was this to continue?

NOTE: See the studies on "The 1260 Years of Persecution" and "The Antichrist."

Daniel 7:26 --------------------- What is going to happen to this power?

Daniel 7:27 --------------------------------- What is God's promise to us?

A Ram and a Goat

Daniel 8

Daniel 8:1-3 -- What did Daniel see?

Daniel 8:4 ---------------------------------- What was this ram doing?

Daniel 8:5 -- What did he see next?

Daniel 8:6, 7 ------------------------------------ What did the goat do?

Daniel 8:8 --------------------- What was to replace the "great horn"?

Daniel 8:20 ----------------------------- What does the ram represent?

NOTE: These kingdoms are the same as those of Daniel 2 and 7. This ram represents the Medo-Persian Empire (as do the silver arms and chest of Chapter 2 and the bear of Chapter 7), which ruled from 538 - 331 B.C.

Daniel 8:21 ----------------------- What do the goat and horn refer to?

NOTE: The goat (as well as the belly and thighs of brass of Chapter 2 and the leopard of Chapter 7) refers to the Greeks who retained power from 331 - 168 B.C. The "notable horn" is reference to Alexander the Great, the first king.

Daniel 8:22 ----------------------------- What was to follow Alexander?

NOTE: After his death Alexander's kingdom was divided between his four generals: Cassander, Lysimachus, Ptolemy, Seleucus.

Daniel 8:23 ---------- When was the fourth kingdom, Rome, to arise?

NOTE: This "king of fierce countenance" vs. 23 and "little horn" vs. 9 parallel the iron legs of Chapter 2 and the dragon-like beast of Chapter 7 in symbolizing Rome in its pagan form, while the "little horn" of Chapter 7 is reference to its papal form.

Daniel 8:24 -- What was it to do?

Daniel 8:25 ----------------------------- Who was it to stand against?

Daniel 8:25 ----------------------------- What was to happen to it?

The Seventy Weeks of Daniel

Daniel 8:27 -------------------------- How many understood the vision?

Daniel 8:1-12 ------------------------------------- What did Daniel see?

Daniel 8:20-22 ------- What did the ram, goat, and horns represent?

Daniel 8:14 -------------------- What was the only thing not explained?

Daniel 9:21-23 ------------------ What did Gabriel return to explain?

NOTE: The vision referred to is Daniel 8 and the only matter not explained is the 2300 days and the cleansing of the sanctuary(vs.14).

Daniel 9:24 -------------- How much time was set aside for the Jews?

Ezekiel 4:6 -------------- What does one day equal in prophetic time?

Daniel 9:25 -------------------- When was this time prophecy to begin?

NOTE: This decree was given by the Persian ruler Artaxerxes in 457 B.C. (Ezra 7:12, 13).

Daniel 9:25 ---- How long after this before the Messiah is anointed?

NOTE: 69 weeks equal 483 years (69x7), which brings us to A.D. 27.

Luke 3:1, 21, 22 ----------------------------- When was Jesus baptized?

NOTE: The fifteenth year of the reign of Tiberius was A.D. 27.

Mark 1:15 ----------------------------- What did Jesus say was fulfilled?

Daniel 9:27 ------- How much of the covenant was left for the Jews?

NOTE: One week would bring us to A.D. 34 (27+7=34).

Daniel 9:26, 27 ------ What happened in the midst of the last week?

Ephesians 2:15 ---------------------- What became of the ordinances?

Colossians 2:14 ------------------------------------ When did this happen?

NOTE: Jesus was crucified in A.D. 31, 3 ½ years after His baptism, and the sacrificial system came to an end (Mark 15:37-38).

Matthew 10:5, 6 -------------------- What did Jesus tell the disciples?

Matthew 21:43 ---------------------------- What did Jesus tell the Jews?

Acts 7:57-8:1 -------- Who was the first Christian martyr in A.D. 34?

Acts 13:46 ---------------------------- What did Paul declare to the Jews?

Romans 2:28, 29;9:6-8 --------------- Who is the Israel of God today?

Galatians 3:26-29 ----------------------- Who are God's people today?

The Cleansing of the Sanctuary

Daniel 8:14 -------- What was to happen at the end of the 2300 days?
NOTE: The Bible only refers to two sanctuaries, one on earth and the other in heaven.

Exodus 25:8, 9 ------------ After what, was he to build the sanctuary?

Hebrews 8:1, 2, 5 --------------- Where is the location of the original?

Exodus 26:33 ----------------------- How many apartments did it have?

Hebrews 9:6 -------------- How frequent was the ministry in the first?

Hebrews 9:7 ---------- How frequent was it in the second apartment?

Leviticus 16:29 ---------------------- When did the high priest do this?

Leviticus 16:30 --- What was he doing?

Leviticus 16:7-9 -- How did he do it?

Leviticus 16:15, 16 ---------------------- What did he do with the blood?

Leviticus 16:20-22 ------------------------ What did he do with the sins?

Leviticus 23:27, 28 ------------------ What were the people to be doing?

Leviticus 23:29, 30 ------------- What happened to those living in sin?
NOTE: Jesus has begun the cleansing of the heavenly sanctuary or the blotting out of the record of confessed sins there, as well as from our lives here.

Revelation 22:11, 12 ------- What pronouncement will He soon make?

2 Thessalonians 1:7-9 ------------ What happens to those still sinning?

1 Thessalonians 4:16, 17 -------------- What happens to the righteous?

Matthew 7:21-27 --------------------- Which group will you be found in?

Revelation 14:7 - What should we be doing in this time of judgment?

Hebrews 4:14-16 -------------------------- What assurance do we have?

The 1260 Years of Persecution

Revelation 12:6 ------------- How long was the church to be in hiding?

Revelation 11:3 ------- How long was God's word to be in mourning?

Daniel 7:25 ----------- How long were God's people to be persecuted?

Daniel 12:7 ------------- How long were God's people to be scattered?

Revelation 12:14 -------- How long was the church in the wilderness?

Revelation 11:2 --- How long was Jesus' heavenly ministry despised?

Revelation 13:5 -- How long was the beast to have undisputed power?

NOTE: We shall now establish that these seven references all refer to the same period of time.

Genesis 7:11 ---------------------------------- When did the flood begin?

Genesis 7:24 ---------------------------------- How long did it continue?

Genesis 8:3, 4 ---------------- When did the ark rest upon Mt. Ararat?

NOTE: From the above verses we discover that a month consists of 30 days. From the seventeenth day of the second month to the seventeenth day of the seventh month (or five months) equals 150 days. Thus the 42 months of prophecy would equal 1260 days (42 months x 30 days = 1260 days). In the Bible a "time" equals one year (Dan. 4:23, 32), "times" equals two years, and "a dividing of time" or "half a time" would equal a half of a year. Thus a time would be 360 days (30 days in a month times 12 months in a year), times would be 720 days (two times 360), and a dividing or half a time would be 180 days (one half of 360) making a total of 1260 days. Therefore, we can readily see that all seven of these passages refer to the same period of time.

Ezekiel 4:6 -------------------- How long does a day equal in prophecy?

NOTE: This 1260 years refers to the period of undisputed power of the "little horn," "beast," "man of sin," or "antichrist" from 538 until it received its "deadly wound" in 1798.

The Antichrist

Six parallels which show that the "little horn" of Daniel and the "beast" of Revelation are the same antichrist power.

1. Both are a blasphemous power ----------------- Dan. 7:25; Rev. 13:6
2. Both make war with the saints ----------------- Dan. 7:21; Rev. 13:7
3. Both have a mouth speaking great things --- Dan.7:8, 20; Rev. 13:5
4. Both were to arise about the time Rome fell - Dan.7:23,24; Rev. 13:2
5. Both were to reign supreme for 1260 years ---- Dan. 7:25; Rev. 13:5
6. After this the Lord's people were to be delivered from persecution and the power was to be led into captivity --- Dan. 7:25; Rev. 13:10

Seventeen identifying points of the antichrist

1. It is a power that was to arise during the time of the kingdoms which immediately followed Rome ------------------------- Dan. 7:24
2. It was to be a "diverse" or different power than any of the previous kingdoms (it was to be religious as well as political) --- Dan. 7:24
3. It was to ascend the throne of the Caesars --------------- Rev. 13:2
4. It was to receive its power and authority from Rome --- Rev. 13:2
5. This power was to destroy three other kingdoms (Heruli, Ostrogoths, Vandals) in its rise to supremacy ----------- Dan. 7:24
6. It was to maintain its power for 1260 years ------------- Dan. 7:25
7. After 1260 years it would receive a "deadly wound" --- Rev. 13:3
8. The wound would eventually be healed --------------- Rev. 13:3, 12
9. During the 1260 years it made war with God's people --- Dan. 7:21
10. It would speak "great things" against God --- Dan. 7:25; Rev. 13:5
11. It was to be guilty of blasphemy ----------------------- Rev. 13:5, 6
12. It would "think" to change God's law and His time --- Dan. 7:25
13. He exalts himself above God -------------------------- 2 Thess. 2:4
14. He claims to be God ---------------------------------- 2 Thess. 2:4
15. Its number "666" is the name or title of a "man" --- Rev. 13:18
16. It is to be an amazing world-wide power ---------------- Rev. 13:5
17. It shall lure many into receiving its "mark" - Rev. 13:6;14:9, 10

The Man of Sin

His Power:

1. "The king shall do according to his will" ----------- Daniel 11:36
2. "Think to change times and laws" --------------------- Daniel 7:25
3. "Power was given him over all... nations" ------- Revelation 13:7

His Self-Exaltation:

1. "He shall exalt himself" ------------------------------- Daniel 11:36
2. "Exalteth himself" ------------------------------ 2 Thessalonians 2:4
3. "Magnify himself above every god" ------------------- Daniel 11:36
4. "He magnified himself even to the Prince of the host" --- Daniel 8:11
5. "He shall magnify himself in his heart" --------------- Daniel 8:25

His Prosperity:

1. "Shall prosper" -- Daniel 11:36
2. "Prevailed against them" ------------------------------- Daniel 7:21
3. "It practiced and prospered" --------------------------- Daniel 8:12
4. "Shall prosper, and practice" -------------------------- Daniel 8:24
5. "He shall cause craft to prosper" ---------------------- Daniel 8:25
6. "Power was given him over all... nations" ------- Revelation 13:7
7. "All that dwell upon the earth shall worship him" ---- Revelation 13:8

His Persecution of God's People:

1. "They shall fall by the sword, and by flame, by captivity, and by spoil many days" ------------------------------------- Daniel 11:33
2. "Made war with the saints" --------------------------- Daniel 7:21
3. "Shall wear out the saints of the Most High" -------- Daniel 7:25
4. "Shall destroy the mighty and the holy people" ----- Daniel 8:24
5. "Shall destroy many" --------------------------------- Daniel 8:25
6. "It was given to him to make war with the saints" --- Revelation 13:7
7. "As many as would not worship the image of the beast should be

killed" --- Revelation 13:15

His Blasphemy:

1. "Speak marvellous things against the God of gods" - Daniel 11:36
2. "A mouth speaking great things" -------------------------- Daniel 7:8
3. "A mouth that spake very great things" ---------------- Daniel 7:20
4. "He shall speak great words against the most High" - Daniel 7:25
5. "There was given to him a mouth speaking great things and blasphemies" -- Revelation 13:5
6. "He opened his mouth in blasphemy against God" - Revelation 13:6

His Opposition to God:

1. "Neither shall he regard the God of his fathers" -- Daniel 11:37
2. "He shall also stand up against the Prince of princes" -- Daniel 8:25
3. "Opposeth and exalteth himself above all that is called God, or that is worshipped" --------------------------- 2 Thessalonians 2:4

His Position as a False God:

1. "He shall magnify himself above all" ---------------- Daniel 11:37
2. "He as God sitteth in the temple of God, shewing himself that he is God" --------------------------------------- 2 Thessalonians 2:4
3. "A god whom his fathers knew not shall be honour with gold, and silver, and the precious stones" ----------------------- Daniel 11:38
4. "And they worshipped the dragon which gave power unto the beast: and they worshipped the beast" --------- Revelation 13:4

His Destruction:

1. "Prosper till the indignation be accomplished" --- Daniel 11:36
2. "The beast was slain, and his body destroyed, and given to the burning flame" --------------------------------------- Daniel 7:11
3. "They shall take away his dominion" ---------------- Daniel 7:26
4. "He shall be broken without hand" --------------------- Daniel 8:25
5. "Shall drink of the wine of the wrath of God" -- Revelation 14:10
6. "Was cast into the lake of fire and brimstone" -- Revelation 20:10

Temperance

2 Corinthians 6:17, 18 ------------------ What does God call us to do?
1 Corinthians 10:31 -------- Will this have an impact on what we eat?
1 Corinthians 3:16, 17 ----------------- What warning does God give?
1 Corinthians 6:19, 20 ------------- Why is this subject so important?
   NOTE: In view of the above principles, one should refrain from the use of things which tend to harm, impede, or shorten one's life; as well as those things which He has strictly forbidden.
Proverbs 23:29-32 ------------- What is God's warning about alcohol?
Isaiah 5:20-22 ---------- Who does the Bible say has woe and sorrow?
Isaiah 5:24 ---------------- What do people do when they use alcohol?
Proverbs 20:1 --------------------- What should we not be deceived by?
1 Corinthians 6:10 ----------------------- Will drunkards be in heaven?
3 John 2 --------------------------------- What does God desire for us?
Isaiah 55:2 -------------------------------------- What are we to eat?
Genesis 7:2 ----- Did Noah realize a distinction between the animals?
Leviticus 11:1-8 ----------------------- How can we tell the difference?
Leviticus 11:9-12 -------------------- What must fish have to be eaten?
Leviticus 11:46, 47 ------------------------ Why did God give this list?
Isaiah 66:15, 16 ------------------------- What event is here referred to?
Isaiah 66:17 ----------------------- Who will be destroyed in that day?
Romans 12:1, 2 ----------------------- What does God want you to do?

Stewardship

Psalm 50:10-12 ---------------------------------- What belongs to God?

Haggai 2:8 -- What else is His?

Psalm 24:1 ------------------------------ What besides this earth is His?

1 Corinthians 6:19, 20 ------ Aside from creation why are we God's?

1 Corinthians 4:2 ---------------------- What is required of a steward?

Leviticus 27:30 ----- What will a faithful steward always remember?

Numbers 18:21 -------------------- What was this tenth to be used for?

1 Corinthians 9:13, 14 ---------------------- What is it used for today?

Proverbs 3:9 -------------------------------------- Which tenth is God's?

Matthew 23:23 ---------------------- What did Jesus say about tithing?

Malachi 3:8, 9 ---- What do we do if we withhold tithe and offering?

Malachi 3:10 -------- What does God want us to "prove" Him about?

Matthew 6:26-32 --------------------- Does He promise to care for us?

Matthew 6:33 --------------- What should be placed first in our lives?

2 Corinthians 9:6, 7 - How much above the tithe is the offering to be?

Matthew 25:21 --------- Don't you want to hear Jesus say this to you?

Christian Adornment

Jeremiah 10:23 --------------------------- The way of man is not where?

Proverbs 16:25 -- Where could it end?

Proverbs 28:26 ------------------------------ What does a fool trust in?

Exodus 35:10 ---------------------------------- What do the wise do?

1 Corinthians 10:31 ------------ In what things are we to glorify God?

2 Corinthians 6:15-18 --------------- What is God's call to His people?

Isaiah 62:10 --------------------- What are we to set before the people?

1 Corinthians 6:19, 20 ---------- What are we and what are we to do?

Exodus 33:5, 6 -------------- What did God tell the people to take off?

Judges 8:24 ---------------------- What identified them as Ismaelites?

Genesis 35:2-4 ------------ What were the ornaments associated with?

Hosea 2:13 --------------------- How does God portray apostate Israel?

Revelation 17:3-5 -------------- How is the corrupt church described?

Isaiah 3:9, 16-23 -------------- What were their ornaments a sign of?

Isaiah 4:4 ---------------------- What does God call their adornment?

1 Timothy 2:9, 10 ------ How should God's people adorn themselves?

1 Peter 3:3-5 ----- What should be the only ornament of a Christian?

1 John 2:15-17 --------------------------------- What are we not to love?

Romans 12:1, 2 --------------------------- What does God want us to do?

1 Thessalonians 5:22 ------------------------------ What are we to avoid?

Titus 2:11-14 ------------------------- What kind of people are we to be?

What Is Sin?

Matthew 1:21 ------- Did Jesus come to save us IN sin or FROM sin?

Isaiah 59:1, 2 --- What does sin do?

Isaiah 1:18 --------------------------------- What does He want us to do?

Romans 6:23 --------------------------- What is the end result of sin?

Romans 6:16-18 ------------------------ What two choices do we have?

> *NOTE: The Bible defines sin as our willful choice to exercise our fallen nature in opposition to the revealed will of God.*

1 John 3:4 --- What is sin?

Hebrews 10:26, 27 --- What is the result of willfully disobeying God?

James 4:17 ------------------------------ How does the Bible define sin?

John 15:22, 24 ------------------- Is there guilt apart from knowledge?

John 9:41 -------------------------------- What brings the guilt of sin?

> *NOTE: None will ever be condemned for not following light they never had.*

Acts 17:30 --------- What types of sin does God not condemn one for?

James 1:14, 15 ------------------------------------- Is temptation sin?

Hebrews 4:15 --------------------------------------- Was Jesus tempted?

1 Corinthians 10:13 --------------------------------- Do we have to sin?

Hebrews 4:16 ------ Where is our power for overcoming temptation?

The Human Nature of Jesus

John 1:1-3, 14 ------------------------- Did Jesus really become flesh?

Hebrews 2:14-17 ----------------------------- Who was He made like?

Romans 1:1-3 ------------------ Who was one of His earthly ancestors?

Romans 8:3, 4 -------- What type of flesh did He take upon Himself?

1 John 4:3 -------------------- What does the spirit of antichrist deny?
  NOTE: The word flesh here always refers to fallen flesh. Never once is it used in reference to unfallen, sinless flesh.

Philippians 2:5-7 ------------ Who was Jesus made in the likeness of?
  NOTE: The phrase "made Himself of no reputation" means literally "emptied Himself." When He became man, He emptied Himself of His Godly powers to meet the Devil on the same ground we must meet him on. These three powers were His omniscience (all knowing), omnipotence (all powerful), and omnipresence (all present).

Mark 13:32 - Did Jesus still know all things while in His human form?

John 5:19, 30 ------- How only was He able to do the things He did?

John 8:28 -------------------- How much was He able to do on His own?

Matthew 26:39, 42 - To Whom did He always keep His will submitted?

Revelation 3:21 -------------------------------- How are we to overcome?

James 4:7 ------------------------------ What are we called upon to do?

Justification

2 Corinthians 1:9, 10 ---------------------- When does God deliver us?

Hebrews 12:2 ---------------------------------- What is Jesus called?

Philippians 1:6 -------------------- Who finishes the work Jesus began?

NOTE: What Jesus did in the past the Bible calls justification, what He is doing in the present is called sanctification, and what He will yet do in the future is called glorification.

Romans 5:18 -------- How many have been justified by Jesus' death?

John 1:29 ------------------------------ Whose sin did Jesus take away?

Hebrews 2:9 -- Who did He die for?

1 John 2:2 ---------------------- How much of the world was justified?

2 Corinthians 5:19 ----------------- Who did He reconcile to Himself?

2 Corinthians 5:14, 15 ---------------------- How many did He die for?

Romans 5:6-8 ------------------------------------ When did He die for us?

Hebrews 2:3 - What can cause us to lose what He has already given us?

Sanctification

1 Thessalonians 4:3 ---------------- What is God's will for His people?
Acts 26:18 -------------------------------- By what are we sanctified?
2 Thessalonians 2:13, 14 ----------- How important is sanctification?
Galatians 2:20 ------------- What is necessary to live a sanctified life?
Romans 6:6-8 ----- What is the result of being crucified with Christ?
Romans 6:1, 2 - Can a person who is dead to sin continue to live in sin?
Romans 6:11, 12 ------------------------ What are we called upon to do?
Colossians 3:1-3 ------ Where should our thoughts and affections be?
Colossians 3:9, 10 ------------- Whose image will we begin to reflect?
Ephesians 4:22-24 ------- What must be renewed for this to happen?
Romans 8:6, 7 ----------- Why is the renewing of the mind necessary?
Colossians 1:21, 22 --- Without this new mind, what will we remain?
Romans 12:1, 2 --------------------- What does Paul call upon us to do?
Philippians 2:5 ------------------------ Whose mind are we to receive?
1 Peter 4:1, 2 ----------- What are we to arm ourselves with and why?
1 Thessalonians 5:23, 24 ------- How complete is sanctification to be?

The Power of the Holy Spirit

Galatians 5:17 ------------ What can we not do, the good or the bad?

Galatians 5:16 ---------------------- What prevents us from doing evil?

Romans 6:14, 16, 18, 20, 22 --------- Can one serve both God and sin?

1 John 4:4 -------------------- Which is greater, the Spirit or the flesh?

Romans 8:1 ---- Who are those in Christ and without condemnation?

Romans 8:8, 9, 14 - If we do not walk in the Spirit, can we be Christ's?

2 Corinthians 3:17, 18 --- What happens as we walk after the Spirit?

Matthew 5:48 -------------------------------- How perfect are we to be?

1 John 3:2, 3 ------- When Jesus comes, will His people be like Him?

1 John 3:6-9 ------------------------ Will God's people continue in sin?

1 John 5:18 ----------------- Will the Holy Spirit lead anyone into sin?

1 Peter 1:15, 16 ------------------------------------ What are we to be?

Ephesians 5:27 ---- What will the church be like when Jesus comes?

Zephaniah 3:13-15 ---------------- What will His people not be doing?

Titus 2:11-14 ---------------------- What is God's desire for your life?

2 Peter 1:3, 4 ------------- Can you believe this wonderful assurance?

The Gift of Tongues

Acts 2:1-6 --------------- How did every one hear the apostles speak?

Acts 2:7-11 -------------------------- Did anyone need an interpreter?

1 Corinthians 12:1-10 -------------------- Do all receive the same gift?
   NOTE: In the modern charismatic movement, it is claimed that all must receive the gift of UNKNOWN tongues.

1 Corinthians 12:7- Are the gifts given to benefit the believer or body?

1 Corinthians 12:11, 18 ------------ Who decides who gets what gifts?

1 Corinthians 12:28 - What place does tongues hold in the list of gifts?
   NOTE: Of the three lists of the gifts of the Spirit (Ephesians 4:11-14; Romans 12:6-8; 1 Corinthians 12-14), only Corinthians lists tongues (and even then at the bottom of the list), and that in seeking to correct a problem that had arisen from a corruption of the true gift.

1 Corinthians 13:1-3 - What is needed for any of these to be effective?

1 Corinthians 14:1, 5 ---------------- Which gift is the most desirable?

1 Corinthians 14:4 --- Why is this greater than an unknown tongue?

1 Corinthians 14:6, 9, 11 - Why should others understand what is said?

1 Corinthians 14:12 ------- What is the primary purpose of the gifts?

1 Corinthians 14:15 ---- What should one always have when praying?

1 Corinthians 14:18, 19 -- What did Paul say about tongues in church?

1 Corinthians 14:22 ---------------------- To whom are tongues a sign?
   NOTE: In the modern charismatic movement, it is taught that the gift of tongues is the sign to the church that one has received the Holy Spirit. This is in direct opposition to what Scripture teaches.

1 Corinthians 14:26, 33 -- What was the apparent problem in Corinth?

1 Corinthians 14:40 -------------------- What is Paul's closing counsel?

Michael the Archangel

Daniel 10:13, 21 --------------------------- Who is Michael said to be?
NOTE: The literal rendering of vs. 13 is "first prince" as the marginal reading shows.

Isaiah 9:6 ----------------------- What is one of the titles given to Jesus?

Acts 5:31 -------------------------------- What is Jesus besides Saviour?

Luke 10:17, 18 ------------------------- What did Jesus say about Satan?

Revelation 12:7-9 ------------------------ Who cast Satan out of heaven?

Jude 1:9 -------------------------------- Who raised Moses from the dead?
NOTE: Archangel is a compound of two Greek words: "arche" which means beginning or commencement, and "aggelos" which means angel or messenger. The word arche is also closely related to the word "archo," which means "to be first" or to "reign (rule) over." Thus the "Archangel" is the One who began (created) the angels and reigns over them. That would be none other than Christ.

1 Thessalonians 4:16 - When Jesus comes, whose voice raises the dead?

John 5:25-29 ------- Whose voice did Jesus say would raise the dead?

Daniel 12:1, 2 ------------ What will happen when Michael stands up?

Revelation 22:11, 12 -------------- What is Jesus soon going to declare?

Matthew 16:27 -------------------------------- Who is coming with Him?

Matthew 24:29-31 ---------------- Are you ready for this glorious day?

Hell

Four words in the Bible have been translated into the English word Hell. The Hebrew word Sheol is found 65 times in the Old Testament and is rendered "hell" 31 times, "grave" 31 times, and "pit" 3 times.

Psalm 89:48 --------------------------- How many who die go to sheol?

Psalm 16:10 ----------------------------------- Who is not left in sheol?

NOTE: This passage in the N. T. uses the Greek word Hades (Acts 2:27). The Greek word Hades is found 11 times in the New Testament and is translated as both hell and grave.

Revelation 1:18 ---------------------- What does Jesus have the keys to?

1 Corinthians 15:55 -------------------- What does hades refer to here?

The word Gehenna is used 12 times and is always translated hell. It is a compound of two words meaning "valley of hinnom" (a place where the garbage or refuse was dumped and burned) and refers to the total destruction of the wicked by fire at the end of the world.

Matthew 5:22 ---------------------------------- What is gehenna called?

Matthew 5:29, 30 --------------------------- What is cast into gehenna?

Matthew 10:28 --- What happens to both body and soul in gehenna?

The Greek word Tartarus is found only once in the New Testament.

2 Peter 2:4 ---------------------------------- Who was cast to tartarus?

Revelation 12:9, 12 ------------------ Where was Satan actually cast?

2 Peter 3:10-12 ------------------------- What will happen to this earth?

2 Peter 3:7 --------------------- When will this destroying fire happen?

2 Peter 2:9 ---------------- When are the wicked punished in this fire?

Matthew 13:40-42 ------------------------------- When will this day be?

Malachi 4:1-3 ------------------------ How consuming will this fire be?

Ezekiel 28:14-19 ------------------------------ What will it do to Satan?

Revelation 20:14, 15 --- What two things are cast into this lake of fire?

Isaiah 47:14 ------------------------------ Will the fire eventually go out?

Isaiah 65:17 ---------------------------------- What will God then create?

2 Peter 3:13, 14 ---------- Knowing all this, what should we be doing?

The Messiah

This study will take the Old Testament prophecies of the Messiah and show the New Testament fulfillment of these in the life and death of Jesus.

The place of His birth ------------------------- Micah 5:2; Luke 2:4-7

His virgin birth ------------------------------- Isaiah 7:14; Luke 1:26-31

The slaughter of the children ----- Jeremiah 31:15; Matthew 2:16-18

His flight into Egypt -------------------- Hosea 11:1; Matthew 2:14, 15

The time of His baptism ------------- Daniel 9:24, 25; Luke 3:1, 21, 22

His rejection by the people ----------------------- Isaiah 53:3; John 1:11

His entrance into Jerusalem ---------- Zechariah 9:9; Luke 19:29-38

His betrayal by a friend -------------------- Psalm 41:9; Luke 22:47, 48

The price of His betrayal ----------- Zechariah 11:12; Matthew 26:15

Spat upon and beaten -------------------- Isaiah 50:6; Matthew 26:67

Crucified between two thieves --------- Isaiah 53:12; Mark 15:27, 28

The wounds in His body --------- Zechariah 12:10; John 19:34; 20:27

His words on the cross ------------------------- Psalm 22:1; Mark 15:34

Given vinegar and gall to drink -------- Psalm 69:21; Matthew 27:34

Gambling for His clothes ------- Psalm 22:17, 18; Matthew 27:35, 36

None of His bones were to be broken --- Psalm 34:20; John 19:32, 33

To be buried with the rich ------------ Isaiah 53:9; Matthew 27:57-60

His resurrection ------------------------------- Psalm 16:10; Luke 24:1-7

The Rapture

John 14:1-3 --------------------------- What did Jesus promise to do?

Matthew 24:36 -------------- What did He say concerning His coming?

Luke 12:37-40 -------------------- What did He say we should be doing?

Revelation 3:3 -- Why did Jesus say we should watch for His coming?

Revelation 16:15 ---------------- Whom did Jesus say would be blessed?

1 Thessalonians 5:1-6 --- Will His coming be a surprise to everyone?
Note: When Jesus comes, the unexpectedness of His coming brings "sudden destruction" upon those who are not ready.

2 Peter 3:10-12 -- Does His coming as a thief mean it will be secret?

Matthew 24:3 ---- What does the Bible say happens when He comes?

Matthew 24:30, 31 -------- What will His angels do when He returns?

Matthew 13:49, 50 -- When are the righteous and wicked separated?

Revelation 6:14-17 ---- What happens to the mountains and islands?

Isaiah 24:20 ----------------- What impact will this have on the earth?

Revelation 16:20 ----------- How drastic of a change will this cause?

1 Thessalonians 4:16, 17 -- What happens to God's people at this time?
NOTE: All of God's people, not just a few, will rise to meet Him when He comes.

1 Corinthians 15:51-53 ------------ How did Paul describe this event?

2 Thessalonians 2:8 -- What happens to the wicked at Jesus' return?

Revelation 1:7 ----------------- How many will witness Jesus' coming?
NOTE: The Bible is very clear that the coming of Jesus will be a literal, visible, audible, eminent event in which He shall be accompanied by all of His holy angels. This glorious event, which will be witnessed by everyone, shall be heralded by shouting and trumpets blowing, and as the earth convulses every island and mountain shall disappear, the righteous dead shall be raised, the wicked shall all be destroyed, the righteous living shall be changed "in the twinkling of an eye," and all of the righteous shall rise "together" to meet the Lord in the air. As can be seen the coming of Jesus will in no way be a "secret," sneaking in and out to snatch just

a few Christians away.

<u>DOESN'T THE BIBLE SAY SOME WILL BE TAKEN AND SOME LEFT?</u>

Matthew 24:37-44 ------- What happened to the wicked at the flood?
NOTE: It was the wicked that were taken away at the flood, <u>not the righteous</u>, and Jesus said this is what will happen when He returns. Therefore, He says, watch and be ready for He will come when the world is not expecting Him.

Luke 17:26-30 -------------------- How does Luke describe this event?
NOTE: Just as there was no second chance at the time of the flood or at Sodom and Gomorrah, there will be no second chance when Jesus comes. These passages clearly reveal that <u>to be taken means to be destroyed</u> and to be left means to be left alive. As with the flood all of the wicked were taken away or destroyed, and only the righteous were left alive. As with Sodom all of the wicked were destroyed and only Lot and his family left.

Matthew 13:27-30, 36-42 ---- When are the good and bad separated?

Revelation 22:11, 12 --- Are you ready for this fateful pronouncement?

Once Saved, Always Saved

John 3:16 ---------- Is salvation based upon belief or predestination?

2 Corinthians 1:9, 10 ---------- Is salvation an ongoing experience?

Philippians 1:6 ----------- What assurance does God's word give us?

NOTE: Salvation is a past, present, and future working of God in the life of the believer.

Galatians 3:3 ----------------- How was this work of salvation begun?

NOTE: The teaching of once saved and predestination go hand in hand. If God has predestinated people to be saved, then it is impossible for them to reject God's irresistible grace and be lost. In other words God chooses some to be lost and others to be saved without any choice or action on their part and nothing can alter their destinies. They are not saved because they have responded to His love, nor lost because they have rejected it, but because God has foreordained them to be saved. But is this what the Bible teaches?

Deuteronomy 30:19, 20 ------- What two choices do each of us have?

Joshua 24:15 ----------- Are we free to choose whom we shall serve?

NOTE: God has given each of us a free will to choose or reject Him and the gift of eternal life.

John 15:2-6, 10 -------------- What does Jesus say each of us must do?

1 John 1:7 --------- What must we continually do to abide in Christ?

1 John 2:24 ------ Is it important we remain faithful to God's word?

John 8:51 ----------- What must a Christian do to have eternal life?

2 Peter 1:10 ----------- What assurance does Peter give the believer?

Romans 8:13 ---------------- What warning does Paul give Christians?

NOTE: Scripture is filled with warnings about falling away and being lost. If God's grace is irresistible, such warnings would be unnecessary. If salvation is based upon God's "irresistible grace," then even faith becomes unnecessary, for God simply chooses whom He will save regardless of any act of faith or response to His love. Therefore, one can live as he or she pleases and still be saved because God has ordained it so. If this is so, then why did not God exercise this "irresistible grace" in the garden of Eden and save this world a lot of trouble, suffering, and heartache?

Hebrews 11:20-22 -- What causes one to be cut off from God's grace?

Hebrews 3:6, 12-14 -------- How long must we hold fast to our faith?

Hebrews 10:26-29 -- What happens when we willfully sin against God?

Hebrews 10:35-38 ----------- What does God's word counsel us to do?

Hebrews 10:39 ------ What two groups of people does Paul contrast?

NOTE: If it were not possible for someone to lose salvation, why would the Bible contain so many warnings about this possibility becoming a reality.

1 Corinthians 9:26, 27 ---- Did Paul realize he could fall from grace?

NOTE: The word "castaway" is found only here in the Bible and comes from the Greek word "adakimos." This word is translated "reprobate"(Romans 1:28) or "rejected" (Hebrews 6:8). The abominable and disobedient are called "adakimos" (Titus 1:16) and Jesus does not dwell in the heart of one who is "adakimos" (2 Corinthians 13:5). This is what Paul said he would become if he did not consciously choose to remain faithful to Christ.

Hebrews 6:4-6 ---- What do those who fall from truth do to Christ?

2 Peter 2:20-22 --- To what does Peter compare those who fall away?

2 Peter 3:14-17 ---- Why are we told to be "diligent" and "beware"?

Revelation 22:19 --- Can one's name be removed from the book of life?

Exodus 32:32, 33 ------ What can cause our names to be blotted out?

Revelation 3:5 --- What will prevent our names from being removed?

Matthew 24:13 ---------------- Whom did Jesus say would be saved?

NOTE: The Bible is clear that believers can choose to be lost as surely as sinners can choose to be saved. If once a person was saved they could never fall, then the devil would not even waste his time on believers, nor would he need to expend his energies on non-believers for they are already his.

1 John 5:11-13 -------------- How can we know we have eternal life?

Why Suffering and Death

Genesis 1:31 ----------------- What was this earth like after creation?

Genesis 3:1-5 ------- What one thing was forbidden Adam and Eve?

Genesis 3:6 ------------------------------- Did Adam and Eve obey God?

Genesis 3:24 -------------- What was the result of their disobedience?

John 8:44 ------------------------------------ What did Jesus call Satan?

Genesis 5:5 ----- What eventually happened to Adam because of sin?

John 14:30 ------------ What is Satan called because of Adam's fall?

Job 2:1, 2 ----------- What gathering did he attend as earth's prince?

Job 2:3-7 -------------------- What challenge did Satan present to God?

Luke 13:16 ------------ Who is it that causes sickness and suffering?

NOTE: From the beginning Satan has brought sickness, suffering, and death to our planet. He is the one behind all the crime, wars, and destruction that are so prevalent today. Even the violence of nature is his handiwork and one of his greatest deceptions, for he has mankind referring to these things as "acts of God." Not only does he bring physical sickness and suffering, but far worse, he brings spiritual sickness and suffering.

Acts 13:6-10 --------- What does he work through people to achieve?

NOTE: Those who are engaged in trying to keep people from finding out what the truth of God's word is, are the children of the devil.

Luke 8:12 ------------ What does Satan seek to take from our hearts?

Matthew 13:24-26, 37-40 --- Who are the two that sow in our hearts?

Luke 22:3, 4 --------------------- What caused Judas to betray Jesus?

NOTE: When anyone betrays Jesus, it is because the devil has entered into them.

Luke 10:18 -------------------------------- Where did Satan come from?

Revelation 12:7-9 ------------- What caused him to fall from heaven?

NOTE: Heaven is a strange place for war to begin, but Satan was there. He has been in the middle of every war since; whether it's a nation, church board, choir, the home, or a marriage. The only way to get rid of the war is to get rid of Satan.

Isaiah 14:12-14 -------------------- What led to his rebellion in heaven?
NOTE: Satan weakens the nations and anything in which he is involved has death and destruction in it. He carries with him the seeds of death and destruction for any program, nation, or person that takes him in.

Ezekiel 28:14-19 -------------- What will eventually happen to Satan?
NOTE: Many wonder "why God didn't destroy Satan during the war in heaven." "If He could speak worlds into existence, couldn't He speak the devil out of existence?" Remember, Satan had made some mighty strong charges. Perhaps he accused God of being unfair or unjust, or that his laws were arbitrary and too restrictive. He may have made the same accusations that many of his disciples make today in trying to get rid of God's law. He undoubtably accused God of being a liar (as he did in the garden of Eden) and said follow me I'll give you something better. His arguments were so convincing that he took a third of the angels with him when he fell. What if God had zapped him out of existence? Can you imagine the impact it would have had on the other angels and the doubts that would have arisen in their minds? "Maybe Satan was right!" "If we are not careful, God will zap us too." Would they have worshiped God out of love and trust or fear? Of necessity, God had to give Satan time to reveal to the universe the true traits of his character. His true character was revealed at the cross when he put to death the Son of God.

1 John 3:8 ---------- For what purpose did Jesus come to this world?
NOTE: All of Satan's works of sickness, suffering, death, crime, wars, destruction, etc. will soon be brought to an end.

Hebrews 2:14 ------ Who shall be destroyed because of Jesus' death?

Revelation 12:12 ----------------- Why is Satan working so hard today?

1 Peter 5:8 --------------------- What must we do until he is destroyed?

Revelation 21:3-5 ------------------------- What is God's promise to us?

Angels - Fact or Fiction

Acts 1:9 -------------- What received Jesus as he ascended to heaven?

Revelation 1:7 ------------ What will accompany him when He returns?

Psalms 104:1-5 -------------- What does the Bible say these clouds are?

Psalms 68:17 --------------------------- What are these chariots of God?

Matthew 25:31 -- How many angels accompany Him when He returns?

Revelation 5:11; Hebrews 12:22 --------- How many angels are there?

Genesis 3:24 ----------------------- Did angels exist before sin and death?

> *NOTE: Angels were in Eden before anyone died, therefore we know they are not the spirits of dead people. They were created before man.*

Hebrews 2:6, 7 -------------- Are angels a different species than man?

Hebrews 13:2 ------- What has resulted from hospitality to strangers?

> *NOTE: The scriptures are filled with accounts of these heavenly beings. They have appeared to men to partake of the hospitality of earthly homes, such as Abraham and Lot (Genesis 18:1-19:26). They have also appeared in their true form as with Jacob at Mahanian (Genesis 32:1, 2), Manoah (Judges 13:2-5), Elijah (1 Kings 19:5-7), Daniel in the lions' den (Daniel 6:22), Cornelius (Acts 10:3-6), Peter in prison (Acts 12:1-10), and hundreds of other encounters.*

Matthew 4:11 ------ Who cared for Jesus in the mount of temptation?

Luke 22:43 ------------------------- Who appeared to give Jesus strength?

Matthew 28:2-6 -------------- Who removed the stone from Jesus' tomb?

Matthew 26:53 -------- Could angels have delivered Jesus from death?

Revelation 12:7-9 -– What happened to some of the angels of heaven?

Isaiah 14:12-14 --------------------------- What was the cause of this war?

Ezekiel 28:13-15 ------------ What position did Lucifer hold in heaven?

> *NOTE: Satan had been one of the two angels that stood next to the throne of God covering it with his wings (Exodus 25:20), but he was not content to stand beside the throne; he wanted to sit in it.*

Ezekiel 28:16-19 ------------------ What will happen to the fallen angels?

Ephesians 6:11, 12 ------- Until that day what are we counseled to do?

2 Corinthians 11:14, 15 ---- Do evil angels impersonate God's angels?

NOTE: Even though a third of the angels followed Satan and were cast out of heaven, two thirds remained faithful to God.

Psalms 103:20, 21 ------- How does the bible describe the holy angels?

Hebrews 1:13, 14 ----- To whom do these angels minister besides God?

Matthew 18:10 --------- What does every child have assigned to them?

NOTE: Every child has a guardian angel appointed to him by the King of heaven to watch over him, to guard and care for him from childhood to the end of life's journey.

Psalms 34:7 ------------- What assurance do we find concerning angels?

NOTE: The angels of God are all about us, even though we may not see them.

Numbers 22:31 ---------- What must happen before we can see angels?

NOTE: If our eyes could be opened to see the invisible messengers of God, how much different might our attitudes and actions be? How much sweeter might our words be? Would your words and conduct have been as it was today, if you had seen your angel standing at your side - listening and recording?

2 Kings 6:16, 17 --- Knowing angels surround us should we be afraid?

The Heavenly City

Hebrews 11:16 ------------------ What has God prepared for His people?

Revelation 21:2 ------------------------------------- Where is this city?

John 14:2 ---------- What has Jesus prepared for us in the city of God?

Revelation 21:9-14 -------------------- How did John describe this city?

Revelation 21:16 ---------------------- How large is the New Jerusalem?

NOTE: The size of the city is said to be "twelve thousand furlongs." A furlong is 1/8 of a mile, thus making the city 1,500 miles in circumference or 375 miles long on each side. This would make the capital of the new earth cover an area as large as Virginia, West Virginia, Pennsylvania, Maryland, Washington D.C., and the western half of Ohio combined.

Revelation 21:17 -------------------- How high are the walls of this city?

NOTE: The walls of the city are 144 cubits high. A cubit can range anywhere from 18 to 21 inches. Taking the smaller figure of 18 inches would make these walls at least 216 feet high or about 20 stories.

Revelation 21:18-20 ------ What are the walls and foundation made of?

Revelation 21:21 --- What does the Bible say the streets and gates are?

Revelation 21:22 --------------------- Why will there be no temple there?

Revelation 21:23 ------------ From where does the city receive its light?

Isaiah 30:26; 60:19, 20; Isaiah 24:23 -- Will there be a sun or moon?

Revelation 21:25; 22:5 ---- Will it ever be dark in the new Jerusalem?

Revelation 21:27 --------------------- Who are the residents of this city?

Revelation 22:1 --------------------- What flows from the throne of God?

Revelation 22:2; Genesis 3:24 -------- What item from Eden is there?

NOTE: This tree is said to bear 12 different types of fruit and to do so once every month. This gives an even further insight to the significance of Isaiah 66:22-23 that all of the redeemed will come together to worship God "from one new moon to another." Not only will there be the weekly Sabbath gathering for worship, but apparently there will be another special gathering once each month around the tree of life.

Revelation 21:2 ---------------- Will this city always remain in heaven?

Revelation 20:9 -- What happens when the city descends from heaven?

2 Peter 3:10; Malachi 4:1-3 -------- How consuming will this fire be?

2 Peter 3:11-13 -- What will God make from the ashes of this planet?

Isaiah 35:1 ------------------------------ What will the new earth be like?

Isaiah 33:24 ------------ Will there be sickness in the earth made new?

Isaiah 35:5, 6 -------------------------- Will any suffer from disabilities?

Isaiah 11:6-9 --------- Will there be any disharmony in the new earth?

Isaiah 65:21, 22 -- What shall we have in addition to our city mansion?

1 Corinthians 13:12 ----------------- Shall we know one another there?

Revelation 21:3-5 -- What is God's promise concerning the new earth?

NOTE: Those who truly love Jesus will one day soon be able to walk with him on golden streets, but in order to walk with him there, we must first walk with him here. The question he asks is: "can two walk together, except they be agreed?" (Amos 3:3). Is your life in agreement with the will of God? Remember, heaven is a prepared place for a prepared people. Won't you begin now to make preparation to become a part of God's eternal family? Heaven is a free gift and is based solely upon our response to God's love and his will for our lives. If you are not standing fully on the side of Christ Jesus, don't you think it is time you changed sides?

The Lord's Supper

Luke 22:7-9 ----- What did Jesus send Peter and John to prepare for?

NOTE: For nearly 1500 years the Passover had pointed to the coming of the "Lamb of God." When Jesus died on the cross, it was fulfilled that "Christ our passover" was sacrificed for us (1 Corinthians 5:7) and all of the feasts and ceremonies which had pointed to his coming ended.

Luke 22:10-14 ---- In what miraculous way were they led to the room?

Luke 22:15 -------- What did Jesus know would soon happen to Him?

Luke 22:24 --------------- What problem existed among the disciples?

Luke 22:25, 26 ------------- What did Jesus tell them they should do?

Luke 22:27 ---------------------------- What did He say He had become?

John 13:4, 5 ------- What did He do to illustrate humility and service?

John 13:6-9 ----------- What did He tell Peter if he did not take part?

John 13:10-12 -------------- Was this a spiritual or physical cleansing?

NOTE: Several things reveal that there is great spiritual significance attached to this act of foot-washing.

1. *Having dirty feet separates no one from Jesus.*

2. *If this had been simply the washing of dirty feet, Jesus would not have told Peter, "what I do thou knowest not now; but thou shalt know hereafter."*

3. *To wash nothing but people's feet does not make them clean all over.*

4. *He washed everyone's feet, but declared one was still not clean, "for he knew who should betray him."*

5. *After washing everyone's feet, His question, "know ye what I have done to you?" would have been both ridiculous and insignificant unless there was a much deeper intent in His action.*

6. *His command: "ye also ought to wash one another's feet. For I have given you an example, that ye should do as I have done to you" reveals a much greater depth than merely the washing of dusty feet.*

7. *Finally, Jesus pronounces a blessing upon those who observe this ordinance.*

John 13:13-15 --- What did Jesus say He had given us by this action?

John 13:17 ------- What did Jesus promise concerning this ordinance?

John 13:21, 22 ---------- What knowledge troubled the heart of Jesus?

Matthew 26:21-23 ------------------- What did the disciples ask Jesus?

Matthew 26:24, 25 ------------------------- What did Jesus say of Judas?

Matthew 26:26-30 ----------- What does the bread and wine represent?

1 Corinthians 11:23-26 --- What two things are this to remind us of?

1 Corinthians 11:27-30 - What happens when one partakes carelessly?

1 Corinthians 11:28 ---------- What should one do before taking part?

Does Grace Abolish God's Law?

Matthew 19:16, 17 -------- What must be done to receive eternal life?
Revelation 12:17; 14:12 --- How are God's last day people described?
Revelation 22:14 --- Who are those who have right to the tree of life?
Romans 3:20 ------------------ What is the purpose of the law of God?
1 John 3:4 --------------------- What is the breaking of the law called?
Romans 4:15 -------------- Would there be sin, if there was no law?
Matthew 5:17, 18 ---------------- Did Jesus do away with God's law?
NOTE: Jesus said, "don't even think I came to destroy the law."
Luke 16:17 ----------- What did Jesus say about changing God's law?
Ephesians 2:15 ------ What was done away with at the death of Jesus?
Colossians 2:14 --------------------- What was blotted out at the cross?
Colossians 2:17 ----------- What was the purpose of these ordinances?
Deuteronomy 31:24-26 - Who wrote this temporary law of ordinances?
Hebrews 9:8-12 ---------- What was to cause these ordinances to end?
Mark 15:37, 38 ------- What happened when Jesus died on the cross?
Matthew 22:37-40 --------- Does love make the commandments void?
NOTE: Jesus is quoting the Old Testament (Deuteronomy 6:5 and Leviticus 19:18) in this passage. He is not giving a new law, but says simply, if we love God supremely, we will not transgress the first four commandments by worshiping false gods, bowing down to images, taking his name in vain, or desecrating his holy Sabbath (Exodus 20:3-11). If we love our fellow man as ourselves, we will not transgress the last six by dishonoring our parents, killing, stealing, committing adultery, lying, or coveting what belongs to another (Exodus 20:12-17). This is why Jesus says upon these two "hang all the law" (Matthew 22:40).
Romans 13:8-10 ----- What is the relationship between law and love?
NOTE: The first four commandments pertain to our relationship with God and the last six to our relationship with our fellow man. Imagine what it would be like if the commandments were gone. There would be nothing wrong with lying, stealing, adultery, killing, idolatry, etc.

Regardless of what some say, it is still a sin to break any one of the commandments of God.

Galatians 3:11 -------------- Does keeping God's law earn us salvation?

Ephesians 2:8, 9 ----------------------------------- How are we saved?

Ephesians 2:8-10 --- Are good works (obedience) evident in the saved?

NOTE: Grace makes us obedient children of God, not rebellious against His law.

Romans 3:28 ---------------- What is the only way we can be justified?

Romans 3:31 ----- Does faith mean we must no longer obey God's law?

Romans 6:14, 15 --------- Does being under grace make us free to sin?

NOTE: Repeatedly, Paul emphasizes that grace makes us law keepers, not law breakers (Romans 3:31; 6:1, 2, 14, 15; 7:7). Grace always leads to obedience, never to disobedience.

Romans 8:3, 4 --- Has the law been kept "for us" or is it to be "in us"?

Galatians 6:6 ------------------------------------ What does true faith do?

James 2:14-20, 26 --------------------------- How important are works?

NOTE: Our works are only the evidence of our faith. The things we do are simply the reflection of what we believe. If our faith does not show obedience to God, it is evidence of being destitute of the grace of God, something to be compared to the belief of Satan and his rebellious angels.

James 2:10, 11 ----- What if someone breaks only one commandment?

NOTE: If a person is going to break one of the commandments, he might as well break them all, for the wages of sin is death, whether we break one or all of them.

James 2:12 ---------- Though saved by grace, by what are we judged?

1 John 5:3 --------------- What is the evidence that we truly love God?

1 John 2:4 ----------- What are the disobedient who claim love called?

Revelation 21:8 -------------------------- Where will all liars be found?

NOTE: Liars are the only group that is prefaced with the word "all."

Revelation 22:14 --- Where will the commandment keepers be found?

John 14:15 --------- If you love God, how does He want you to show it?

Books by the Author

1888 - The Message, the Mystery, and the Misconceptions
A historical background and brief overview of the message of righteousness by faith.

Did God send a special message to His people over 100 years ago? Was the message accepted or rejected? What was this message? Can we know it today or did God allow it to be lost for all eternity?

Bible Studies Made Easy
Outline studies of many of the great doctrines of the Bible presented in a clear and concise manner.

An excellent tool for personal study or for sharing your faith.

Dealing With the Devil's Deception - How to Choose a Bible
An overview of the development and dangers of the modern translations of the Bible and the men and motives behind them.

Over four and a half centuries ago the great reformer, Martin Luther, said, "No greater mischief can happen to a Christian people than to have God's word taken from them, or have it so falsified that they no longer have it pure and clear. God grant that we and our descendants be witnesses of such a calamity."

Is it possible that we, today, are witnessing just such a calamity? The answer and issues will become extremely clear when you finish *Dealing With the Devil's Deception*.

God's Last Message to Earth
A simple, yet systematic, verse-by-verse study of the book of Revelation.

Many claim the book of Revelation cannot be understood and that it was never intended to be. The very title of the book, however, refutes this claim, for it is a revelation or revealing.

There is so much in this book God would have His people come to understand that they might prepare themselves and shape their course of action, so as to escape the plagues that are to shortly fall upon the world. His promise is "Blessed is he that readeth, and they that hear the words of this prophecy, and keep those things which are written therein" (Revelation 1:3).

The Secret of the Rapture: Will You Be Left Behind?

Since publication of the *Left Behind* series of books and the recent release of the movie *Left Behind*, there has been an explosion of interest in the sensational and speculative errors being promoted by the movie and the books upon which it is based. This has resulted in many being deceived into thinking these false (and admittedly fictional) concepts are actually Bible truth. The Secret of the Rapture is designed to offset these false and fanciful theories and enable people to see the beauty and truth of the coming of Christ. This little book will strengthen your understanding and faith concerning the "blessed hope, and the glorious appearing of the great God and our Saviour Jesus Christ" (Titus 2:13), as well as enable you to share this great Bible truth with those who are being deceived by the errors being propagated today.

Simplified Studies of the Sacred Scriptures
Question and answer studies of many of the great doctrines and prophecies of God's word presented in a simplified and easy-to-understand format.

This 296 page book is an excellent tool for personal study or Bible study classes. It is filled with Scripture to provide you with answers to nearly all your questions on Bible topics.

Which Gospel?
A treatise of "the everlasting gospel" and how it has been and is being perverted within Christianity.

The word of God makes it clear that the gospel "is the power of God unto salvation." But do we truly understand what the gospel is or the power it has for us today? With the prevailing perversions of the gospel today, can the people of God really discover which gospel contains this life changing power and how to experience it. This book presents the truths of the gospel in such a way as is seldom seen in the Christian world today, revealing God's purpose in the plan of salvation from the atonement to the reception of the redeemed. From justification to the future of God's Remnant church, this book reveals the power of the Holy Spirit and the assurance that what God has promised, He is able also to perform.

The Wise Shall Understand

A verse-by-verse study of the book of Daniel presented in a simple, easy-to-understand manner.

Of all the books of the Bible, Daniel speaks repeatedly of last day events and claims to pertain directly to the "time of the end" (Daniel 12:4, 6, 8, 9, 13). The things written in Daniel were written specifically for those of us living today. Now, as never before, it is necessary for us to understand this book. As for those who say it cannot be understood, I would caution them to beware, lest they find themselves calling God a liar, for He has declared in no uncertain terms that "none of the wicked shall understand; but the wise shall understand" (Daniel 12:10).

Audio, video, and printed material are available on numerous other great Bible teachings. For more information concerning any of these, please contact:

Fourth Angel Ministries
P.O. Box 136637
Ft. Worth, TX 76136
817-919-7267
Fourthangelbooks@aol.com
www.fourthangelministries.com